Mom's Journal

Mom's Journal

WHAT I WANT YOU TO KNOW ABOUT ME AND MY LIFE

JENNIFER BASYE SANDER

Skyhorse Publishing

Skyhorse Publishing books may be purchased in bulk at special discounts for sales promotion, corporate gifts, fund-raising, or educational purposes. Special editions can also be created to specifications. For details, contact the Special Sales Department, Skyhorse Publishing, 307 West 36th Street, 11th Floor, New York, NY 10018 or info@skyhorsepublishing.com.

Skyhorse® and Skyhorse Publishing® are registered trademarks of Skyhorse Publishing, Inc.®, a Delaware corporation.

Visit our website at www.skyhorsepublishing.com.

10 9 8 7 6 5 4

Library of Congress Cataloging-in-Publication Data is available on file.

Cover design by Abigail Gehring

Print ISBN: 978-1-5107-4250-5

Printed in China

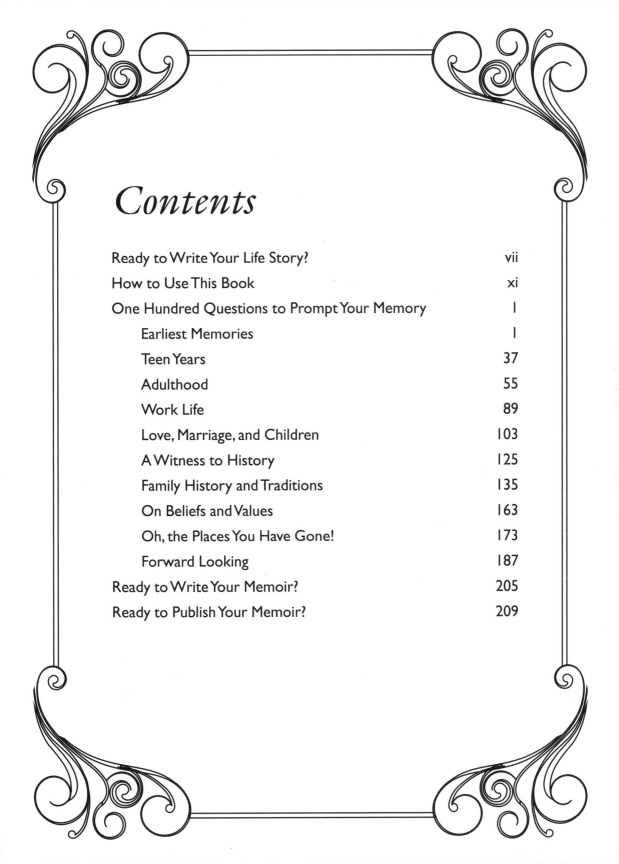

Contents

Ready to Write Your Life Story?

Are you ready to work on the story of your life? There are so many reasons that compel us at some point to sit down and try to put our story on paper. We might be trying to make sense of it ourselves, we might worry that our family stories and traditions might be lost, or there might be information we want our descendants to have. Whatever your reason, now is the perfect time to start. We live in a day and age where it is perfectly normal to work on a personal project. Perhaps when you were younger you were taught that it was impolite to talk about yourself, but those times have passed and now is the time to share. In fact, your younger family members will consider it odd if you don't! They might talk about updating their Facebook page, and now you can say that you need to update your keepsake book page.

Writing about yourself may make you feel awkward or shy initially, but do remember this is your own private material and it will only be seen by the people you care to show it to. You might start off by working on it only when you are by yourself, avoiding the chance that someone in the room might ask what you are writing. Or perhaps you are not at all worried and are ready to let the world know just what you are up to. Go ahead and sit in full view of your family and friends and scribble away on these pages. Don't be surprised if someone peeks over your shoulder, curious to see what you might be putting down.

Where exactly does one start? At the beginning, with your very first memories of childhood? In the middle, when you begin to have adult experiences? Or should you start where you are now in life, and work backwards? There are so many entry points in a life, so many stories to relay. The following pages have a variety of questions to prod your memory and get you to remember details. You will soon be filling page after page with your recollections.

This book is filled with questions to help you get started because writers typically run dry at some point as they stare out the window twiddling their pens. Or as they rearrange the objects on their desks for the hundredth time and dust off their laptop screens. Or as they wish the phone would ring and create a reason to get up and answer it. Any minute now, the creativity is sure to kick in and they will get back to work. . . . Prompts help ease writers past these sticky moments. They give writers an immediate assignment—*here, write about this!* The imagination starts working right away instead of spending all that time waiting to get started on the writerly task at hand.

When answering these questions you might close your eyes and go back in time to try to remember as much detail as you can. Was it hardwood or a carpeted floor you stood on in your grandparents' parlor? Was the radio on? Were there sounds from outdoors? This is your chance to be a reporter on your own life. With every question, stop and think who, what, when, where, why? If each of these requires two or three sentences, soon enough you will have filled the whole blank page and turned to the next one to continue writing. This is your chance to write about life from your own unique perspective.

One thing to keep in mind with everything you put down in black and white to be read by others is this crucial question: How might this make someone feel after you are gone? Answer yourself truthfully. Are you putting something down on paper that should be discussed with someone now, something that might have the power to hurt in the future? Be truthful and honest, but balance it with an eye toward your readers' feelings. You might decide that some of what you want to write needs to be brought up in conversation while you have the chance.

Let's move on to the next phase, then, and get started on writing about your life.

How to Use This Book

Okay, ready to begin? Get yourself a favorite pencil or pen and then . . . but wait. Is there a right way to do this? A wrong way? Do you have to start on the first question and work steadily through each one, not moving on to the next until each one is finished? And what if there is a question you hate? What if it simply doesn't apply to your life?

This is not a life test. There is no right way or wrong way to fill in these pages. You might want to sit down with the book first and flip through to see if there is something that sparks your attention right away. If so, start there. You might spot some uncomfortable questions as you flip through. Perhaps as you get more comfortable with the process you will want to tackle those later, or you might ultimately decide to just ignore them. It is totally up to you.

So go ahead and take the plunge. Pick up that pen. Sharpen that pencil. Start thinking about your life and how you have lived it. Start thinking about what you'd like to pass on to future generations. Start thinking about what moments you'd like to savor and experience for a second time as you write them down here for all to enjoy.

One Hundred Questions to Prompt Your Memory

Earliest Memories

Do you remember the very first time you tried to ride a bike? Where were you? Was it your bike or an older sibling's? Who was teaching you how to ride it?

_____

_____

_____

_____

_____

_____

_____

_____

_____

_____

_____

_____

_____

_____

_____

"Before too long I am going to have to write Chapter One." —John Steinbeck

Did you grow up around brothers and sisters?
Describe them as though to someone who has
never met them before.

I have one sibling a sister named
Sandra. She is the brain of the
family. She's always been the
(the) responsible one. When
we were kids I remember
playing in the pool with her
and pretending we were doing
the final lift in dirty dancing
She would do makeovers
and play dress up with me.
She left the house when I
was 13 our relationship
got even better. I wanted
to help her when she became
a mum and had aliana

_Flip through a family photo album and
describe a scene or a person in detail. Use
it as a jumping-off point . . ._

Can you remember your great-grandparents?

If not, why not? Where were they? In another country?

Do you remember any stories you heard about them?

i never met my great gram parents they pessen away becre i was born.

Just think, if you only answered one of these questions a day you could complete it all in just over three months. Why not set aside a half an hour a day to complete the task?

Everyone loves pie, cookies, and cake, fresh from the oven.
Can you remember being given a special gift of baked goods?
A birthday cake? Cookies after school? Who was with you?
Where did you eat it?

Something I looked foward to
was my birthday pie my mum
would get me from Icecream
cottage

Chris bought me a birthdaycak.
when we were dating and
surprised me at a resurant. it
had Kidial Kat design on it and
when I saw it I cried. I never
had anyone do that for me.

Julia Child once wrote in a letter to a friend: "People who love to eat are always the best people." Relax and enjoy the experience of writing about food, about cooking and eating and sharing.

What did you think of your mother's cooking? Did she have a prized recipe? What did the house smell like when she cooked it? Where did she make it, in what location? Can you describe the kitchen? Did your father cook too?

_____

_____

_____

_____

_____

_____

_____

_____

_____

_____

_____

_____

_____

_____

"Smell is a potent wizard that transports you across thousands of miles and all the years you have lived." —Helen Keller

Did you play an instrument when you were young?

Was it something you enjoyed?

_____

_____

_____

_____

_____

_____

_____

_____

_____

_____

_____

_____

_____

_____

_____

_____

_____

Is there a difference between autobiography and memoir? Memoir comes from the French word for memory or reminiscence. Autobiography comes from the Greek words auto and bio, which mean self and life.

Do you remember stories your parents told you when you were young? Did they tell you stories at night, or sing songs to you? Can you still sing those songs or tell those same stories in detail? Where do you think your parents learned them?

_____

_____

_____

_____

_____

_____

_____

_____

_____

_____

_____

_____

_____

_____

_____

Truman Capote liked to write
"horizontally." The prolific English
romance writer Barbara Cartland liked
to lie down on a couch and dictate her
books to a secretary. So perhaps you too
should try writing while prone.

How clearly do you remember your friends from grade school? Who were they? Did they live nearby? Did you stay in touch with them as the years went by?

_____

_____

_____

_____

_____

_____

_____

_____

_____

_____

_____

_____

_____

_____

_____

_____

A blank page is daunting. Go ahead and
doodle a bit on the edges to get the ink
flowing through your pen, and then the
words will follow.

What do you remember about your toys from early
childhood? Did someone make them? Were they gifts?
Hand-me-downs from another child?

_____

_____

_____

_____

_____

_____

_____

_____

_____

_____

_____

_____

_____

_____

_____

_____

_Writers work best under deadlines. So set
one for this project and try to meet it._

Whether pleasant or unpleasant, smells can trigger very strong memories. Are there particular smells that remind you of childhood, or earlier parts of your life?

_____

_____

_____

_____

_____

_____

_____

_____

_____

_____

_____

_____

_____

_____

_____

_____

_____

_____

_____

_____

_____

_____

_____

_____

_____

_____

_____

_____

_____

_____

Is there a memoir writing group that you can join in your area? Ask at the library or senior center, or investigate a college extension course.

Do you have a favorite fable or fairy tale? Is it from your own childhood or one you discovered reading to your own children? What is appealing about the story?

_____

_____

_____

_____

_____

_____

_____

_____

_____

_____

_____

_____

_____

_____

_____

Try writing in the third person and see what happens. Instead of "I" and "me" on the page, what happens when you tell your stories and refer to yourself as "he" or "she"? You could also try writing from another point of view entirely. What if you told a story from your childhood from the viewpoint of your own mother or father? You might see what happened in a whole new light . . .

What were you afraid of as a child? A disease? The dark?
Something in your home?

_____

_____

_____

_____

_____

_____

_____

_____

_____

_____

_____

_____

_____

_____

_____

_____

_____

_____

_____

_____

_____

_____

_____

_____

_____

_____

_____

_____

*No writer starts at the top, and no writer
is ever really happy with what they have
written. Stephen King wrote his first books
on a large desk made from an old door.
Discouraged, he threw the manuscript for
Carrie away in the trash. His wife fished it
out. In the years since then his novels have
sold more than 350 million copies.*

Were there any colorful characters in your childhood?
Some wild neighbor or memorable relative?

_____
_____
_____
_____
_____
_____
_____
_____
_____
_____
_____
_____
_____
_____
_____
_____
_____

_____

_____

_____

_____

_____

_____

_____

_____

_____

_____

_____

_____

_____

_____

_____

_____

Why not choose a story from your childhood
and turn it into a personalized children's
book for your grandchildren? Perhaps one
of them can illustrate it.

Did you have pets as a child? Is there one memorable story
about a family pet?

_____
_____
_____
_____
_____
_____
_____
_____
_____
_____
_____
_____
_____
_____
_____
_____

Why not draw a picture to add to your story. Try to diagram a room from your childhood home, or sketch a favorite animal.

Were you ever called by a nickname as a child?

How did you feel about it?

_____

_____

_____

_____

_____

_____

_____

_____

_____

_____

_____

_____

_____

_____

_____

_____

_Why not get a friend to work on this
project at the same time? You could sit
at the same table working on the same
question and both get your memoirs done
in no time at all._

Is there an object or memento from your childhood that you wish you still had? Why don't you still have it?

_____

_____

_____

_____

_____

_____

_____

_____

_____

_____

_____

_____

_____

_____

_____

Write down your dreams first thing in the morning. You will be stunned to see how fluid and creative a writer you are, a screenwriter, that is, when your brain isn't even trying.

The story you tell most often about your own childhood is . . .

Remember the difference between fiction
and nonfiction. Fiction is the product of
imagination and invention. Nonfiction
relates to actual events, facts, and
information.

What language or languages did you grow up hearing in your house? In your neighborhood? Do you speak any of those languages today or wish you did?

_____

_____

_____

_____

_____

_____

_____

_____

_____

_____

_____

_____

_____

_____

_____

_____

_____

_____

"It is a delicious thing to write, to be no longer yourself but to move in an entire universe of your own creating."
—Gustave Flaubert

TEEN YEARS

Describe your favorite outfit from when you were a teenager.
Why did you like it so much? Where did it come from?
Where did you wear it?

_____

_____

_____

_____

_____

_____

_____

_____

_____

_____

_____

_____

_____

_____

_____

_____

_____

_____

_____

_____

_____

_____

_____

*Marcel Proust began writing because the
taste of a small cookie brought it all back
to him. Perhaps you can send yourself back
in time by baking a cake and sitting in a
nearby room as the sweet smell fills the air,
or by cooking your mother's favorite dish
on the stovetop.*

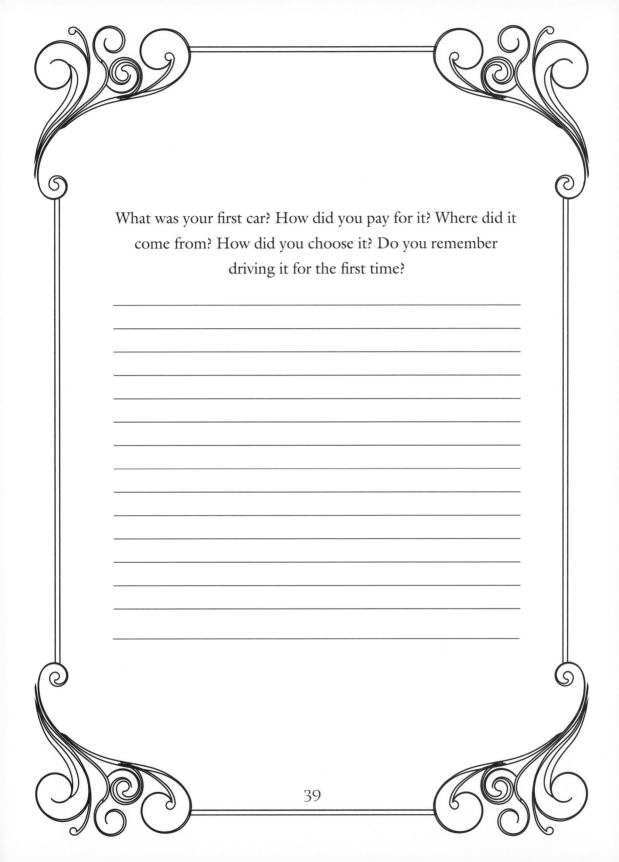

What was your first car? How did you pay for it? Where did it come from? How did you choose it? Do you remember driving it for the first time?

_____

_____

_____

_____

_____

_____

_____

_____

_____

_____

_____

_____

_____

_____

Why not start a private family blog and send one of these stories out to your family members each week?

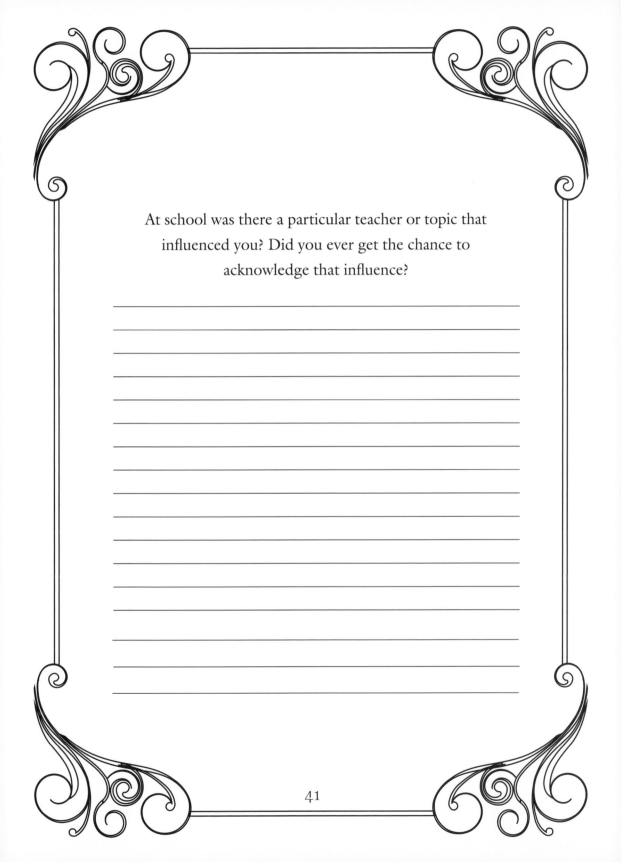

At school was there a particular teacher or topic that
influenced you? Did you ever get the chance to
acknowledge that influence?

Ernest Hemingway liked to work stand-
ing up, and used a desk designed for that
purpose. If sitting at a table or computer
desk doesn't work for you, get up and try a
different place or a different position.

How clearly do you remember your friends from high school? Who were they? Did they live nearby? Are any of them still in your life now?

_____

_____

_____

_____

_____

_____

_____

_____

_____

_____

_____

_____

_____

_____

_____

_____

_____

_____

_____

_____

_____

_____

_____

_____

*Worried about what other people might
say about the way you remember things?
Chances are they will remember it
differently, so just understand that and
go ahead and write it the way you want.
Frank McCourt won the Pulitzer Prize for
his memoir* Angela's Ashes. *It recounts his
hardscrabble childhood in Ireland and
depicts dramatic poverty and hunger.
After it was published his own mother
objected to what he described; she felt he
exaggerated.*

Are there any outlandish fashion items you once wore that make you blush now to remember? A silly fad from high school or college?

_____

_____

_____

_____

_____

_____

_____

_____

_____

_____

_____

_____

_____

_____

_____

_____

_____

_____

_____

_____

_____

_____

_____

_____

_____

_____

_____

_____

_____

_____

Remember, you are now a reporter on your own life. With every question you are answering in these pages, stop and think who, what, when, where, why? Try for several sentences for each one. Before you know it, a paragraph is there on the page before you!

How did you learn best in school? By reading? Experiencing? Listening? Was learning easy for you in school? Or were there challenges you had to overcome?

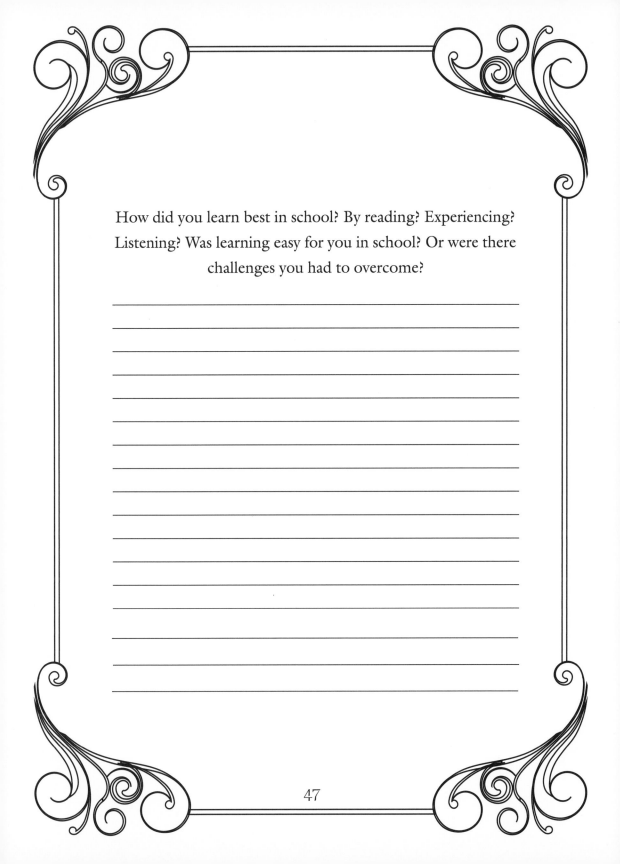

"I cannot live without books."
—Thomas Jefferson

Were you ever in a school or amateur performance? A play or a skit or a singing performance? What do you most remember about it?

_____

_____

_____

_____

_____

_____

_____

_____

_____

_____

_____

_____

_____

_____

_____

_____

_____

Pretend you are having a conversation
with someone who was also at the event you
are describing.

Is there a product, television show, or famous personality that used to be common in your youth but no longer is? What do you miss from the corner grocery store?

_____

_____

_____

_____

_____

_____

_____

_____

_____

_____

_____

_____

_____

_____

_____

_____

_____

_____

_____

_____

_____

_____

_____

_____

_____

_____

_____

_____

_____

_____

Use this project as an excuse to actually revisit your childhood. Pack it up and head back to your hometown.

Is there a book or movie from your adolescence that has stayed with you all of these years? Where and when did you first discover it? Why has it stayed with you?

_____

_____

_____

_____

_____

_____

_____

_____

_____

_____

_____

_____

_____

_____

_____

_____

Listen to music from when you were
younger, or from the era you are describing.

Adulthood

Do you remember the very first time you ever held a baby?
Was it a younger sibling? A niece or nephew? Or one of your
own children? What do you remember about that first
moment?

Why not use this project as a good excuse to organize a family reunion? You could put out the word that you want to hear from everyone about their memories of your ancestors.

Is there anything you think you did *too much* of in your life?

_____

_____

_____

_____

_____

_____

_____

_____

_____

_____

_____

_____

_____

_____

_____

_____

_____

_____

_____

_____

_____

_____

_____

_____

_____

_____

_____

_____

_____

_____

_____

_____

_____

"Nothing is worth more than this day."
—Goethe

Is there anything that you now feel you did *too little* of
in your life?

_____

_____

_____

_____

_____

_____

_____

_____

_____

_____

_____

_____

_____

_____

_____

_____

_____

_____
_____
_____
_____
_____
_____
_____
_____
_____
_____
_____
_____
_____
_____
_____
_____
_____

*"A book itself repeatedly tries to kill its
author during its composition."*
—Michael Chabon

Who would you describe as your heroes? Living or dead? Real or fictional? Pick three and describe why you find them heroic.

_____

_____

_____

_____

_____

_____

_____

_____

_____

_____

_____

_____

_____

_____

_____

_____

_____

_____

Mark Twain's early attempt to have a book published was rejected, and years later that publisher admitted to Twain that, "My chief claim to immortality is the distinction of having declined your first book."

Are there any regrets that weigh on you now?

Is there any way to overcome that?

_____

_____

_____

_____

_____

_____

_____

_____

_____

_____

_____

_____

_____

*Take a walk by yourself and let your
mind wander. You just might
remember something that needs
to be added to one of
your stories.*

What do you regard as the most difficult period in your life?
Why? Was there a war on? Money struggles?
A career setback? Family problems?

_____

_____

_____

_____

_____

_____

_____

_____

_____

_____

_____

_____

_____

_____

_____

Eavesdrop on a conversation at some point today, and then try to write it down verbatim at a later point. How much could you remember? Will that help you remember conversations from years ago?

Was there a moment in your life when you suddenly realized you were an adult?

_____
_____
_____
_____
_____
_____
_____
_____
_____
_____
_____
_____
_____
_____
_____
_____
_____

_____

_____

_____

_____

_____

_____

_____

_____

_____

_____

_____

_____

_____

*What is a copyright? "The right of authors
to control the reproduction and use of their
creative expressions that have been fixed in
tangible form," according to*
The Associated Press Stylebook and
Briefing on Media Law.

What time period of your adulthood have you most enjoyed?

_____

_____

_____

_____

_____

_____

_____

_____

_____

_____

_____

_____

_____

_____

_____

_____

_____

"It takes courage to grow up and become
who you really are." —*e. e. cummings*

Do you have a special skill or trait or talent that might come as a surprise to other people? Something that only you know about?

_____
_____
_____
_____
_____
_____
_____
_____
_____
_____
_____
_____
_____
_____
_____
_____

_____
_____
_____
_____
_____
_____
_____
_____
_____
_____
_____
_____
_____
_____
_____

*"I am myself the matter of my book. You
would be unreasonable to spend your
leisure on so frivolous and vain a subject."
—Michel de Montaigne*

What do you consider the best idea you ever had?

_____

_____

_____

_____

_____

_____

_____

_____

_____

_____

_____

_____

_____

_____

_____

_____

_____

_____
_____
_____
_____
_____
_____
_____
_____
_____
_____
_____
_____
_____
_____

Carry a notebook to jot down memories
or thoughts as they come to you during
your day.

How would you describe your favorite hobbies
and leisure activities?

_____

_____

_____

_____

_____

_____

_____

_____

_____

_____

_____

_____

_____

_____

_____

_____

"I spent the morning putting in a comma,
and the afternoon taking it out."
—_Oscar Wilde_

Is there a particular talent or skill that you wish you possessed? Why? How would you use it?

_____

_____

_____

_____

_____

_____

_____

_____

_____

_____

_____

_____

_____

_____

_____

_____

_____

_____

_____

_____

_____

_____

_____

_____

_____

_____

_____

_____

_____

_____

"I hate writing. I love having written."
—Dorothy Parker

Ever wished you could be someone else, lead someone else's life? Who would it be? Why would you want their life?

_____

_____

_____

_____

_____

_____

_____

_____

_____

_____

_____

_____

_____

_____

_____

_____

_____

Now that you are a writer, you can hang around bookstores browsing or lounge around reading a book and call it working. Or research, anyway.

If you could have one superpower, what would you choose?
Is there a real-life situation in which you could have used it?

_____

_____

_____

_____

_____

_____

_____

_____

_____

_____

_____

_____

_____

_____

_____

_____

_____

_____

_____

_____

_____

_____

_____

_____

_____

_____

_____

_____

_____

_____

_____

What makes a good storyteller? Think about what it is you like or dislike in someone's storytelling style and apply it to your own.

If you were going to be stranded on a desert island for a year,
what would you pack to bring with you?

_____

_____

_____

_____

_____

_____

_____

_____

_____

_____

_____

_____

_____

_____

_____

_____

_"Gratitude is the fairest blossom which
springs from the soul."_
—Henry Beecher Ward

What do you do when no one is looking? Sing? Dance?
Write poetry?

_____

_____

_____

_____

_____

_____

_____

_____

_____

_____

_____

_____

_____

_____

_____

_____

_____

_____

_____

_____

_____

_____

_____

_____

_____

_____

_____

_____

_____

_____

_____

_____

_____

_____

_____

*"If we all did the things we are capable of,
we would astound ourselves."*
—Thomas A. Edison

Is there a dream spot or dream house that you wished you'd lived in?

_____

_____

_____

_____

_____

_____

_____

_____

_____

_____

_____

_____

_____

_____

_____

_____

_____

Feel free to paste in pictures, mementos,
newspaper clippings, or whatever you'd like
to add to the story or to decorate a page.

WORK LIFE

Do you ever feel like you should have had an alternative
career to the one you had? What would it have been?
Why didn't you pursue it earlier in life?

_____

_____

_____

_____

_____

_____

_____

_____

_____

_____

_____

_Prolific French novelist Honoré de Balzac
reportedly drank as many as fifty cups of
black coffee a day to keep writing._

Did you make any lasting friendships during your career
in business?

_____

_____

_____

_____

_____

_____

_____

_____

_____

_____

_____

_____

_____

_____

_____

_____

_____

_If you can work in public, go ahead and
give it a try. Let people wonder just what it
is you are over there in the corner
working on . . ._

Was there a business idea or invention that
you never acted on?

_____

_____

_____

_____

_____

_____

_____

_____

_____

_____

_____

_____

_____

_____

_____

_____

_Writing about business isn't dull. Some of
the bestselling nonfiction books, like Walter
Isaacson's book about Steve Jobs, have been
about the work world._

Did you choose your profession, or did it choose you?
Did your parents or grandparents influence that choice?

_____

_____

_____

_____

_____

_____

_____

_____

_____

_____

_____

_____

_____

_____

_____

_____

_____

_____

_____

_____

_____

_____

_____

_____

_____

_____

_____

_____

_____

_____

_____

_____

*"I never did a day's work in my life. It was
all fun." —Thomas A. Edison*

Over the course of your working career have there been major
changes in your industry? For the better?
What prompted the change?

_____

_____

_____

_____

_____

_____

_____

_____

_____

_____

_____

_____

_____

_____

_____

_____

_____

_____

_____

_____

_____

_____

_____

_____

_____

_____

_____

_____

_____

_____

_____

_____

_____

_____

*"Vision is the art of seeing what is invisible
to others."* —Jonathan Swift

Would you like to see your grandchildren pursue a similar
career? Why? Why not?

_____

_____

_____

_____

_____

_____

_____

_____

_____

_____

_____

_____

_____

_____

_____

_____

_____

_____
_____
_____
_____
_____
_____
_____
_____
_____
_____
_____
_____
_____
_____
_____
_____
_____

*"Tell me and I forget, teach me and
I remember. Include me and I learn."*
—Benjamin Franklin

Do you remember the first money you ever earned?
Who hired you, and what was the experience like?

_____

_____

_____

_____

_____

_____

_____

_____

_____

_____

_____

_____

_____

_____

_____

_____

_____

_____

_____

_____

_____

_____

_____

_____

_____

_____

_____

_____

_____

_____

_____

_____

_____

_____

"Eighty percent of success is showing up."
—Woody Allen

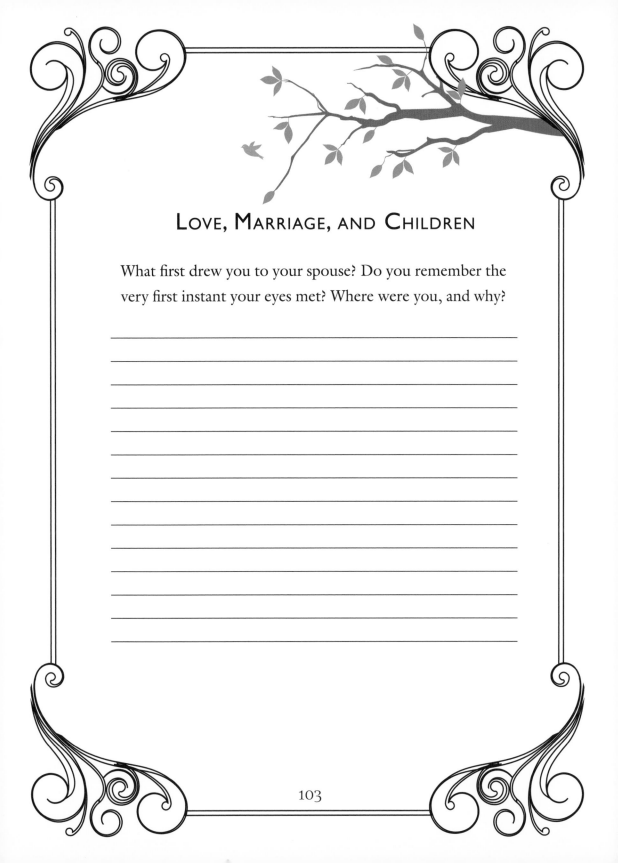

Love, Marriage, and Children

What first drew you to your spouse? Do you remember the very first instant your eyes met? Where were you, and why?

_____

_____

_____

_____

_____

_____

_____

_____

_____

_____

_____

_____

_____

_____

Should you write out your answers on another piece of paper first before copying them into this book? If it suits you. But remember, what you are creating doesn't have to be perfect. Your family wants to know what you know and have experienced, they will not judge the way it is presented.

What do you remember most about your wedding day?

_____

_____

_____

_____

_____

_____

_____

_____

_____

_____

_____

_____

_____

_____

_____

John Grisham wrote his first book on large yellow legal pads, sneaking in time during slack moments in the courthouse. He wrote his second book, The Firm, on a desk wedged between the washer and the dryer in the family laundry room.

What do you consider the high points about marriage?

_____

_____

_____

_____

_____

_____

_____

_____

_____

_____

_____

_____

_____

_____

_____

_____

"Happiness isn't something you experience;
it's something you remember."
—Oscar Levant

What do you consider the low points?

What did you do to get through them?

_____
_____
_____
_____
_____
_____
_____
_____
_____
_____
_____
_____
_____
_____
_____
_____
_____

_____

_____

_____

_____

_____

_____

_____

_____

_____

_____

_____

_____

_____

_____

_____

"Times are bad, children no longer obey their parents, and everyone is writing a book." —Cicero, circa 43 BC

Did you ever regret not apologizing properly to your spouse about something?

_____
_____
_____
_____
_____
_____
_____
_____
_____
_____
_____
_____
_____
_____
_____
_____
_____
_____

The prolific author of the James Bond books, Ian Fleming, would devote his winter visit to Goldeneye, his house in Jamaica, to writing one entire book. He'd start every day with an ocean swim, then eat breakfast, kiss his wife, and head off to write for three hours. He'd return again late afternoon at five for another hour and a half at the task.

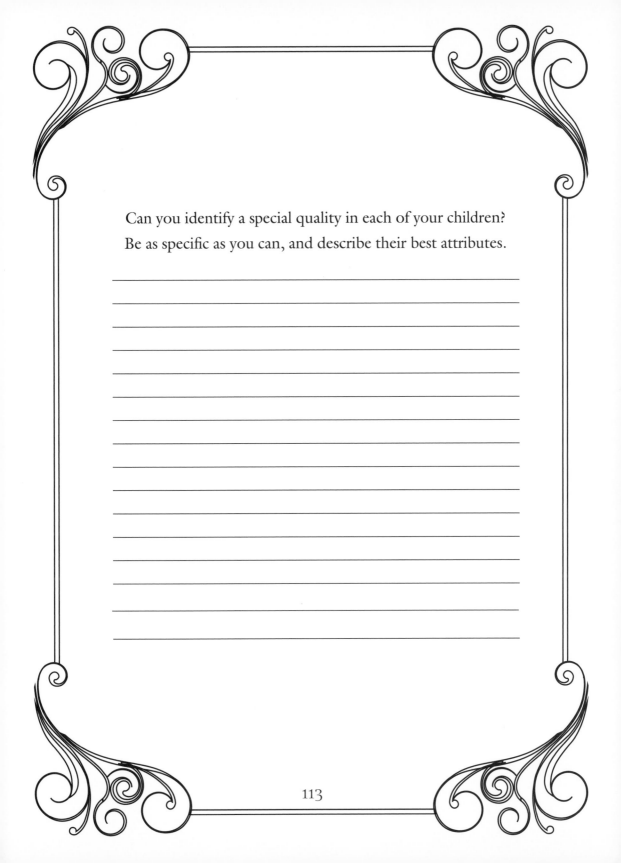

Can you identify a special quality in each of your children?
Be as specific as you can, and describe their best attributes.

Jane Austen wrote Pride and Prejudice
_and most of her other works in a corner of
the family sitting room while the life of the
household went on around her._

Is there anything you wish you'd said to your children when they were young?

_____

_____

_____

_____

_____

_____

_____

_____

_____

_____

_____

_____

_____

_____

_____

_____

Are there any questions you'd like to answer again? Go ahead and go back and write another version. It might be better the second time, or you will think of a different way to approach the same information. Go ahead and tuck in extra pages to this memory book wherever you need them.

What part of being a parent did you most enjoy?

_____

_____

_____

_____

_____

_____

_____

_____

_____

_____

_____

_____

_____

_____

_____

*Writers are not always the most
attentive parents. About Charles Dickens
as a father, his son Charley observed, "The
children of his brain were much more real
to him at times than we were."*

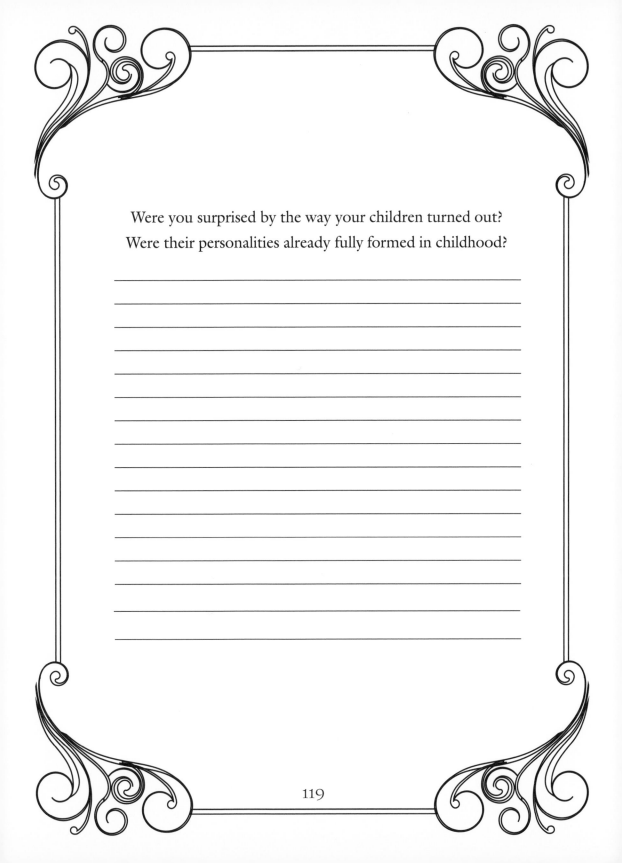

Were you surprised by the way your children turned out?
Were their personalities already fully formed in childhood?

_____

_____

_____

_____

_____

_____

_____

_____

_____

_____

_____

_____

_____

_____

_____

_____

_____

_____

_____

_____

_____

_____

_____

_____

_____

_____

_____

_____

_____

_____

*"The world is full of magic things,
patiently waiting for our senses to grow
sharper." —William Butler Yeats*

Describe your children as babies. Happy babies? Good
sleepers? Was there a moment when you realized they were
no longer babies?

_____

_____

_____

_____

_____

_____

_____

_____

_____

_____

_____

_____

_____

_____

_____

"Laughter and tears are both responses to frustration and exhaustion. I myself prefer to laugh, since there is less cleaning up to do afterward." —Kurt Vonnegut

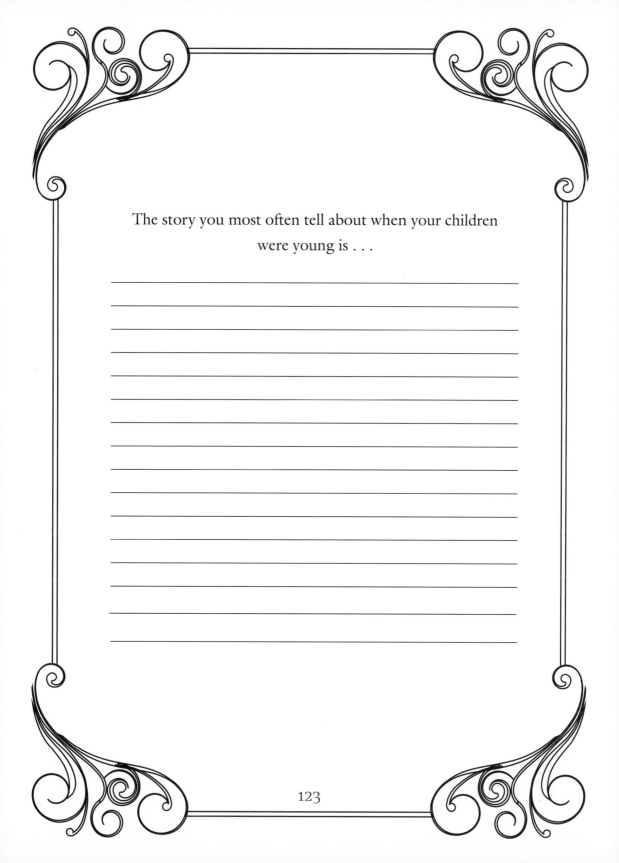

The story you most often tell about when your children
were young is . . .

_____

_____

_____

_____

_____

_____

_____

_____

_____

_____

_____

_____

_____

_____

_____

_____

_____

Give yourself a break from writing about yourself and your own life and look out the window instead. Spend a few minutes just writing about what you see. Take a nature walk from where you are sitting.

A Witness to History

If you could only choose one thing, what would you say is the
biggest change you have witnessed in your lifetime? Was it a
change in transportation, or the way business gets done?
A political upheaval? A scientific or medical breakthrough?

"Life is either a grand adventure or nothing." —Helen Keller

Have you ever been caught in a dramatic or catastrophic
weather situation? What happened? Where were you?

in the Bahammas whenddidIwent
I went on a cruise we were
on a catermaran in the middle
ofthe oceon very Chppy and
wavey

_____

_____

_____

_____

_____

_____

_____

_____

_____

_____

_____

_____

_____

_____

_____

"Every moment and every event of every man's life on earth plants something in his soul." —*Thomas Merton*

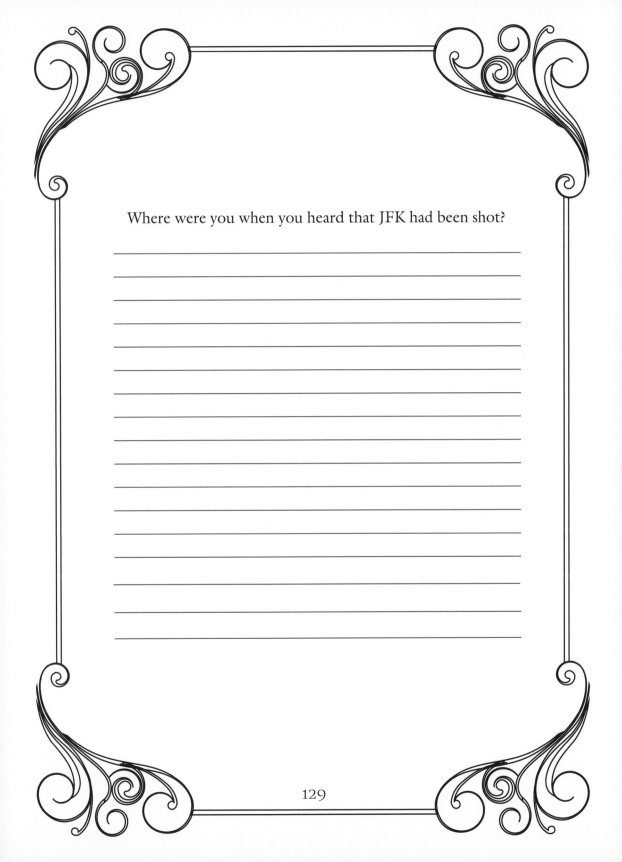

Where were you when you heard that JFK had been shot?

_____

_____

_____

_____

_____

_____

_____

_____

_____

_____

_____

_____

_____

_____

_____

_____

_____

_____
_____
_____
_____
_____
_____
_____
_____
_____
_____
_____
_____
_____
_____

*Yes, of course you can fill out this
entire book. As Teddy Roosevelt
once said, "Believe you can and
you're halfway there."*

Is there a president or world leader from your lifetime whom
you have most admired?

_____

_____

_____

_____

_____

_____

_____

_____

_____

_____

_____

_____

_____

_____

_____

_____

_____

_____

_____

_____

_____

_____

_____

_____

_____

_____

_____

*Churchill drank whiskey while writing.
On the other hand, Hemingway didn't
drink at all when writing. Pour yourself
a little something if that will help you
relax on the page. But if you have a little
too much, better check the next day to make
sure what you wrote under the influence is
really what you want to be
preserved for the ages.*

Ever had a longing to meet an historical or popular figure?

What did you want to talk to them about?

What did you hope to learn?

_____

_____

_____

_____

_____

_____

_____

_____

_____

_____

_____

_____

_____

_____

_____

_____

_____
_____
_____
_____
_____
_____
_____
_____
_____
_____
_____
_____
_____
_____

Stuck halfway through the question? Don't worry too much; put your pen down and try again later, or move to a different question and work on that. There is no time limit here.

Family History and Traditions

Are there family traditions from when you were young that you remember in detail? Anything your family did that other families didn't? Do you have a favorite tradition that you tried to keep alive as the years have passed?

_____

_____

_____

_____

_____

_____

_____

_____

_____

_____

_____

_____

Your children and grandchildren will always be curious about the lives of those who came before them. Give them as much detail as you can, names, faces, places. They might want to use the details someday for a family research project. There is no such thing as too much family history.

Do you have a favorite holiday? What are some childhood memories of that holiday? Memories from your adult life?

_____

_____

_____

_____

_____

_____

_____

_____

_____

_____

_____

_____

_____

_____

_____

_____

_____

_The word "publish" used to mean
to make available in printed form.
Now it can mean simply hitting
"send" and making your words and
thoughts available online._

Is there a trait or talent that you feel you inherited from
your parents?

_____

_____

_____

_____

_____

_____

_____

_____

_____

_____

_____

_____

_____

_____

_____

_____

Whom are you writing for? In your mind
choose a young family member and
pretend you are telling them a story.

Was there a phrase, expression, or word that your parents used often? Did you end up using it too? What do you think your children would say when asked that question about you?

_____

_____

_____

_____

_____

_____

_____

_____

_____

_____

_____

_____

_____

_____

_____

_____

_____

_____

_____

_____

_____

_____

_____

_____

_____

_____

_____

_____

_____

_____

_____

"Writer's block? That's just another word
for lazy." —Robert Parker

Did you inherit anything health-wise from your parents or
grandparents? What do you know about their health that you
can pass along to your family members?

_____

_____

_____

_____

_____

_____

_____

_____

_____

_____

_____

_____

_____

_____

_____

_____

_____

_____

_____

_____

_____

_____

_____

_____

_____

_____

_____

_____

_____

_____

*Self-publishing used to be a bit
down-market, but is now considered
quite ordinary and admirable. So don't
be too shy to give it a try if you'd like to see
more of your life story in book form.*

Describe three things you learned from your own mother.
Have you passed that same knowledge down
to your children?

_____

_____

_____

_____

_____

_____

_____

_____

_____

_____

_____

_____

_____

_____

_____

_____

_____

_____

_Of the fifteen slots on the combined
print and ebook bestsellers on a
recent_ New York Times _list, a total of
eight of the titles were memoirs._

Describe three things you learned from your own father. Have you passed that same knowledge down to your children?

_____

_____

_____

_____

_____

_____

_____

_____

_____

_____

_____

_____

_____

_____

_____

Many successful authors started out publishing their own work. Mark Twain, Ernest Hemingway, Emily Dickinson. Go ahead and give it a try if the idea appeals to you; who knows where it might lead?

Is there a meaningful piece of furniture in the house you'd like to pass on? What should future generations know about it?

_____

_____

_____

_____

_____

_____

_____

_____

_____

_____

_____

_____

_____

_____

_____

_____

_____

_____

_____

_____

_____

_____

_____

_____

_____

_____

_____

_____

_____

_____

_____

_____

*Every day novelist John Cheever would put
on a suit and ride the apartment elevator
down to the storage room where he worked.
Why not get dressed up in your finest to
work on your life story?*

Are there meaningful artworks or pictures that you'd like to
see kept in the family? Why?

_____

_____

_____

_____

_____

_____

_____

_____

_____

_____

_____

_____

_____

_____

_____

_____

_____

_____

_____

_____

_____

_____

_____

_____

_____

_____

_____

_____

_____

_____

_____

*Writing down so many of your memories
and reminiscences might inspire you
to take the next step as a writer and try
your hand at fiction. Go ahead and have
fun turning one of your anecdotes into
a short story with a plot, pacing,
characters, dialogue, and resolution.*

In what way did your parents' lives and experiences shape
who you turned out to be?

_____

_____

_____

_____

_____

_____

_____

_____

_____

_____

_____

_____

_____

_____

_____

Prolific English novelist Anthony Trollope paid a servant an extra five pounds a month to wake him up at 5:30 a.m. and bring him a cup of coffee. Trollope worked for the next three hours, and then headed to his day job at the post office. The result of his diligence? A total of forty-seven published novels.

Is there one character trait that best describes your family? Something that you saw in your parents and grandparents and can see in yourself and your children?

Strength.

_____
_____
_____
_____
_____
_____
_____
_____
_____
_____
_____
_____
_____
_____
_____

"Nothing happens of itself. I believe all
events are produced by will."
—William Burroughs

Are there any family secrets you want to share that would cause no harm in passing along now?

_____
_____
_____
_____
_____
_____
_____
_____
_____
_____
_____
_____
_____
_____
_____
_____

_Asking a sibling or relative to confirm
your facts? Don't be surprised if they
remember it differently. We all filter
things through our own experience._

What was the single best piece of advice you ever got from a family member? Can you describe the occasion on which it was given to you?

_____

_____

_____

_____

_____

_____

_____

_____

_____

_____

_____

_____

_____

_____

*The "memoir" category on Amazon.com's
online bookselling site lists 218,672 results,
of which the memoir* The Glass Castle
*comes up first (even though it was
published years ago).*

If you had the chance to talk to your own parents one more time, what would you say?

_____

_____

_____

_____

_____

_____

_____

_____

_____

_____

_____

_____

_____

_____

_____

_____

_____

_____

_____

_____

_____

_____

_____

_____

_____

_____

_____

_____

_____

_____

_____

_____

_____

*Pretend you are writing a letter. Better yet,
pretend you are writing a letter that no
one else will ever read, that you will never
send. Open yourself up and really let go.*

ON BELIEFS AND VALUES

Has religion played a big part in your life? Would you hope
that it plays the same kind of role in your descendants' lives?

_____

_____

_____

_____

_____

_____

_____

_____

_____

_____

_____

_____

_____

_____

*"If you want God to laugh, tell
him your plans."*
—Woody Allen

Do you have a political belief or philosophy that would
come as a surprise to your family and friends?
Has it evolved over time?

_____

_____

_____

_____

_____

_____

_____

_____

_____

_____

_____

_____

_____

_____

_____

In order to write his speeches and books,
Winston Churchill dictated to a shorthand
writer, speaking slowly and whispering
to himself *sotto voce while trying out
different words and phrases and then
speaking loudly to the secretary when he
at last found the right thing.*

What happens after we die?

_____
_____
_____
_____
_____
_____
_____
_____
_____
_____
_____
_____
_____
_____
_____
_____
_____

_____

_____

_____

_____

_____

_____

_____

_____

_____

_____

_____

_____

_____

*"Life is like riding a bicycle. To keep your
balance you must keep moving."
—Albert Einstein*

What matters to you most? A person, a thing, an idea, a philosophy? Albert Einstein once said, "A table, a chair, a bowl of fruit, and a violin; what else does a man need to be happy?" Expand on this with your own requirements, or respond to Einstein's own list.

_Norman Mailer worked for years in the
attic of his Cape Cod home at a desk
with his back to the view out the window.
Dwayne Raymond, in_ Mornings with
Mailer, _his charming memoir of working
as Mailer's literary assistant in the years
before the author's death, says that it was
an intentional choice to avoid distraction._

How do you describe yourself in one word when you meet someone new? Is it regional, political, or ethnic? For instance, as a Californian, Republican, or Irish? Why does that identity trump all others?

_____
_____
_____
_____
_____
_____
_____
_____
_____
_____
_____
_____
_____
_____
_____

_____

_____

_____

_____

_____

_____

_____

_____

_____

_____

_____

_____

_____

_____

Mark Twain paid to publish Ulysses S. Grant's memoirs. Ezra Pound paid to publish one of Ernest Hemingway's first books. Everyone starts somewhere, and sometimes another writer can help.

OH, THE PLACES YOU HAVE GONE!

Is there one place that was your favorite vacation spot?

_____
_____
_____
_____
_____
_____
_____
_____
_____
_____
_____
_____
_____
_____

_____

_____

_____

_____

_____

_____

_____

_____

_____

_____

_____

_____

_____

_____

"It's not what you look at that matters,
it's what you see."
—Henry David Thoreau

What was your favorite family vacation when you were a child?

_____

_____

_____

_____

_____

_____

_____

_____

_____

_____

_____

_____

_____

_____

_____

_____

_____

_____

_____

_____

_____

_____

_____

_____

_____

_____

_____

_____

_____

"I grow old . . . I grow old . . . I shall wear
the bottoms of my trousers rolled."
—T. S. Eliot

What was the most memorable vacation you took with your own children?

_____
_____
_____
_____
_____
_____
_____
_____
_____
_____
_____
_____
_____
_____
_____

_____

_____

_____

_____

_____

_____

_____

_____

_____

_____

_____

_____

_____

_____

_____

_____

"I'd rather regret the things I've done than regret the things I haven't done."
—Lucille Ball

Is there a place you wanted to travel to but never got the
chance? Why did you want to go there?
Why didn't you get to go?

_____

_____

_____

_____

_____

_____

_____

_____

_____

_____

_____

_____

_____

_____

_____

_____

_____

_____

_____

_____

_____

_____

_____

_____

_____

_____

_____

_____

_____

_____

_____

_____

_____

_____

*Use this project as an excuse to travel.
Take yourself and this book somewhere
quiet for the weekend.*

Have you attended many live musical or theatrical
performances? Who was with you,
and where did you see them?

_____

_____

_____

_____

_____

_____

_____

_____

_____

_____

_____

_____

_____

_____

_____
_____
_____
_____
_____
_____
_____
_____
_____
_____
_____
_____
_____

"What did they expect? I'm a writer, I use everything." —Truman Capote, after his glamorous friends realized he was writing about them and abandoned him

Can you describe a memorable restaurant meal? Where were you dining? Who was with you? Why were they there, too?

Is there someone you love to sit next to at a
dinner party? Is there someone you avoid
at all costs?

Do you have a favorite natural season, or time of the year?
What most appeals to you about it? Is there a place you like to
go to enjoy it?

_____

_____

_____

_____

_____

_____

_____

_____

_____

_____

_____

_____

_____

_____

_____

_____
_____
_____
_____
_____
_____
_____
_____
_____
_____
_____
_____
_____

*"Someone's sitting in the shade today
because someone planted a tree long ago."*
—Warren Buffett

FORWARD LOOKING

What keeps you up at night? What do you consider the biggest challenge facing future generations? Do you have any words of advice for them?

_____

_____

_____

_____

_____

_____

_____

_____

_____

_____

_____

_____

_____

_____

_____

_____

_____

_____

_____

_____

_____

_____

_____

_____

_____

_____

_____

_____

_____

_____

_____

_____

"We are made wise not by the recollection of our past, but by the responsibility for our future." —George Bernard Shaw

What would your ideal funeral service look like? How would you most like to be remembered? Is there anything you don't want your friends and family to do then? Do you have legal documents or instructions for your family?

_____

_____

_____

_____

_____

_____

_____

_____

_____

_____

_____

_____

_____

_____

_____

_____

_____

_____

_____

_____

_____

_____

_____

_____

_____

_____

_____

_____

_____

_____

_____

_____

*"It is true that we are called to create a
better world. But we are first of all called
to a more immediate and exalted task:
that of creating our own lives."*
—*Thomas Merton*

If your children inherit any money from you, how would you like them to best spend their inheritance? What do you think extra money should be used for? Is there any use that you would absolutely disapprove of?

_____

_____

_____

_____

_____

_____

_____

_____

_____

_____

_____

_____

_____

_____

"If you get stuck, get away from your desk. Take a walk, take a bath, go to sleep, make a pie, draw, listen to music, meditate, exercise; whatever you do, don't just sit there scowling at the problem."
—Hilary Mantel

What are your hopes for your grandchildren?

_Never let yourself get hung up on the
need for perfection. Your family will
remember you for your stories, not for your
punctuation and grammar._

If you ruled the world, what is the one big thing you would change and why?

_____

_____

_____

_____

_____

_____

_____

_____

_____

_____

_____

_____

_____

_____

_____

_____

_____

_____

_____

_____

_____

_____

_____

_____

_____

_____

_____

_____

_____

_____

_____

*Give yourself a party when you are finished
with this project. Your guests can take
turns reading out loud from the pages.*

Have you made the world a better place by your presence here on earth? What do you consider your single greatest contribution?

_____
_____
_____
_____
_____
_____
_____
_____
_____
_____
_____
_____
_____
_____
_____
_____

_____

_____

_____

_____

_____

_____

_____

_____

_____

_____

_____

_____

_____

_____

_____

*"I, not events, have the power to make
me happy or unhappy today. I can choose
which it shall be. Yesterday is dead,
tomorrow hasn't arrived yet. I have just
one day, today, and I'm going to be happy
in it." —Groucho Marx*

If you had a sudden financial windfall, what type of charity would you most like to fund?

_____

_____

_____

_____

_____

_____

_____

_____

_____

_____

_____

_____

_____

_____

_____

_____

_____

_____

_____

_____

_____

_____

_____

_____

_____

_____

_____

_____

_____

_____

_____

_____

*"Your worth consists in what you are and
not in what you have."*
—*Thomas A. Edison*

Is there a modern day invention that you consider dangerous? Something you would prefer the world be without?

Social media

_____

_____

_____

_____

_____

_____

_____

_____

_____

_____

_____

_____

_____

_____

"Don't judge each day by the harvest you reap but by the seeds you sow."
—Robert Louis Stevenson

Is there anyone you'd like the chance to apologize to? Why?
Why haven't you done it before?

_____

_____

_____

_____

_____

_____

_____

_____

_____

_____

_____

_____

_____

_____

_____

_____

_____

"Life's tragedy is that we get old too soon
and wise too late."
—Benjamin Franklin

Ready to Write Your Memoir?

I hope you enjoyed the process of remembering incidents from long ago, relating family stories that need to be preserved, and offering up your thoughts on a variety of topics. You worked long and hard, and certainly deserve to take a much-needed break from this project.

But what if you feel you are just warming up? If this question-and-answer format has helped you start to write about your life, is there a way to keep going? Of course. You can easily take what you have here and turn it into a more formally structured memoir or autobiography.

Writing a memoir sounds like a daunting task, but understand that you have now done quite a bit of the hard stuff—the research, the sifting through memories and mementos and describing just what you remember. You have one hundred ways to expand your book, one hundred paths to explore. How ever to organize it? Let's look at a few ways you can do that.

Have you ever said these words: "When I get around to writing my life story, I'm going to call it . . ." You might already have decided long ago just what you would call the book. And perhaps the title of your proposed book will help you decide how to organize the material and what exactly to focus on. For instance, when Ted Robinson sat down to write his memoir about his experiences during World War II, he called it *Water in My Veins*.

Taking a look at just one individual year is a literary device often used by memoir writers. *Paris in Love* focuses on just one year during which a family of four moved from suburban New Jersey to Paris. Starting with their move overseas and working through the school year as an organizing principle, it is not the entire history of a family, just one short year. *A Year by the Sea* is a look at one year in the life of a woman who decides not to accompany her husband on his latest corporate job transfer, but rather to live alone in their summer cottage at Cape Cod. Was there one critical year in your life that could form the basis for a book?

Or perhaps your title will reflect some of the people you focus on in your memoir. Maya Angelou has written a book called *Mom & Me & Mom*. It is divided into two equal parts, the first half, *Mom & Me*, focuses on her relationship with her mother when she was a child. The second half, *Me & Mom*, focuses on their later relationship when Maya was herself an adult. In a similar vein, Carol Burnett has released a memoir called *Carrie and Me: A Mother-Daughter Love Story*. In the case of both, a reader knows what is in store—not an entire life story of the author but rather just the life stories that illustrate one important relationship.

Don't yet have a title in mind? Don't let that hold you back. Here are a few other ways that you can organize your material and start to put your personal story into a longer form.

Chronological: Think of this as the yearbook approach. Go back through all of your questions and assign years to everything. The first time you held one of your own babies? Was that the same year as when you moved into your first house? Or was that the year that you had that big job transfer?

Write out a list of years and then start brainstorming about things that happened then. Should you decide to use this kind of a structure to write about your life and start from day one until the present time, it would be considered more of an autobiography than a memoir. One is not better than the other; they are simply different types of writing and give the reader a different type of experience. You can also take a bigger chunk of time and organize by decade. The forties, the fifties, and so on.

Object Memories: The author Bill Bryson wrote a wonderful book called *At Home* in which all he really did was wander about his own house looking at various parts of it and investigating the history. *Why do houses have chimneys?* he wondered, as he stood in front of his, before launching into an investigation of the history of chimneys.

You can use this same technique too, and create a memoir that jumps around in time and space by focusing on one small thing—a family photo, a well-used coffee mug, or your grandfather's rocking chair—and then using that as the start of a longer reminiscence. Flip back through the hundred questions. So much of what you would need to use this technique is already there.

Cameos: Rather than trying to weave together everyone in your life, you can instead devote entire sections to writing about just one person at a time. Perhaps you want to start with your grandparents or parents and write down everything you'd like to pass along about them, regardless of the year it happened or where you were in the story. You might want to start with your children and write on that experience first before drawing back as though you were holding a camera and revealing the other people in the picture.

Themes: You might also decide only to write about one big theme or topic. Instead of writing about your life from day one you might instead write only about your WWII years, or the story of your marriage, or perhaps a memoir about your business career.

Places: George Howe Colt wrote *The Big House: A Century in the Life of an American Summer Home* about his family's longtime place on Cape Cod. Woven into the story of the house are the stories of his family. Is there a house in your life that has played a large role? A summer rental that your family and friends have returned to year after year? Could you tell a larger story by focusing just on what happened there year after year?

Ready to Publish Your Memoir?

Now that you have launched into writing your life story as a memoir or autobiography, do you think you'd like to see it someday as an actual book? Something that you can proudly present to your family and friends? Or perhaps even something that might have a wider audience? Now doubt you have been hearing how easy it is nowadays to self-publish and have wondered if that might be the route for you.

Publishing copies of your personal memoir in book form is a lovely idea. Just think how amazing it would be to hold a copy of a book you wrote in your hands. A book with a cover that uses pictures or artwork meaningful to you. The path you take to having a finished book depends on what your ultimate goals are. Is it purely a personal project for friends and family, or do you have your heart set on bringing your story to a larger audience? If it is a purely personal project, then relax and enjoy the process.

Turning your manuscript into a book involves several steps. You must first have someone else read your work and look for errors in spelling, punctuation, or grammar. Many memoir writers turn to someone in their circle for this step, but it is always valuable to have your work examined by a professional who will be more clear-eyed about the work. Once the manuscript is ready, it needs an interior design. All of the major do-it-yourself publishing sites have standard designs you can use. Next, you will need a cover. You might want to use artwork from a grandchild, photos from your life, or other symbolic ways to convey a message about your life. This part of the process can be very creative and enjoyable.

Alright, who are you going to use to produce the actual book now? Two of the top self-publishing companies are Createspace.com (owned by Amazon.com) and DiggyPOD.com. Diggy POD lets you compare their prices and services with other major companies and claims to have the best value. Be wary when dealing with any of the self-publishing sites; they might work hard to convince you to upgrade from the amount you intend to spend and sign up for much fancier levels of editing and production. They might also want to sell you a website for your book, or help with marketing and publicity. Hang on to your wallet throughout the process.

Are you feeling overwhelmed by the thought of producing a book? There are other ways to get your story out to a wider audience. What about a video of you telling stories? It is so easy to do nowadays; each one of us has a video camera in our hands at all times with iPads and iPhones. Your grandchildren would love to be asked to produce something with you.

What about recording your memories in your own voice and giving out copies of a disc or audio file to those with whom you'd like to share?

Regardless of whether you decide to take your memories into another form, stop and savor the feeling that you have produced a lasting record of who you are, where you came from, and what you believe. Congratulations; that is an accomplishment worth celebrating.